THE EPISTEMOLOGY OF LOSS

Early Praise for *The Epistemology of Loss*

❖

"Donald Wolff's *The Epistemology of Loss* collects thirty-eight poems and arranges them in five movements that give the collection a mature and sophisticated architecture. The volume earns word by word, line by line, form by form, its right to speak to all of us. Wolff reminds us, with both self-deprecating humor and a resilient sadness, what's at stake if we don't find the right words. His expansive, balanced vision takes us deeply into the perilous way of the world and guides us cautiously out again, the journey all but complete—and well worth our studied attention. It's a fine, rich, and complex book."

—GEORGE VENN, Author of *Lichen Songs:*
New and Selected Poems

❖

"*The Epistemology of Loss* is marked by the sense it gives of a person talking intimately, a hard thing to make so natural. It's a different book each time I read it and I think I've caught up to the central theme of the collection—how perilous life is, and how precious for that reason. There's something very encouraging about the way love emerges from tragedy and near tragedy in so many of the pieces. They speak to us with close assurance and commitment."

—PAUL MERCHANT, Translator with Michael Faletra of
Unless She Beckons: Poems of Dafydd ap Gwilym
presented in Welsh and English

❖

redbat books
pacific northwest writers series

the Epistemology of Loss

poetry by

DONALD WOLFF

redbat
books

redbat books
La Grande, Oregon
2022

© 2022 by Donald Wolff

All rights reserved.

Printed in the United States of America

First Edition: June 2022

Trade Paperback ISBN: 978-1-946970-07-7

Library of Congress Control Number: 2022941363

Published by
redbat books
La Grande, OR 97850
www.redbatbooks.com

Text set in IM FELL English PRO and Garamond Premier Pro

Cover photos by
ksummers and jak/morguefile.com

Book design by
redbat design | www.redbatdesign.com

Table of Contents

Acknowledgements

The author wishes to express his gratitude to the editors of the following journals and anthologies for first publishing these poems:

Aspects of Robinson: Homage to Weldon Kees: "In the Way of the World"
basalt: "Red-Tailed Hawks"
Blue Collar Review: "What's Coming"
Cloudbank: "Early," "The Rhetoric of Bees and Stone"
Conestoga Zen: "San Juan Island Respite"
Gold Man: "Eastern Oregon Triptych"
Miramar: "In the Blood," *Entrance to Paradise*, "This White Monday,"
    "Winter Light," "Catching Up with Evolution"
Packinghouse: "Even Now," "What's Close to Me"
SALT: "Just between Us," "Middle Two Rock Road," "Asymmetry"
Solo Nova: "Simultaneity"
Teeth of the Wind: "Close Encounters"
Writing Home: An Eastern Oregon Anthology: "Along the Snake,"
    "Ladd Marsh in Poor Weather"

pro familia et amicis

I. Just between Us

Along the Snake

While I wade up to my chest down river
from the Oxbow Dam, a deer stands
knee deep beneath the concrete bridge
to pull at leaves from the hanging
branches, the water all we have
in common besides the air. My children
jump from that bridge twenty feet down,
bob up swimming first to one pylon,
then another, and back to shore.
My daughter had to build up to it
time and time again until she finally
leaped falling straight through space
arms flat against her sides, toes pointed
to slice into the water, her courage
borrowed from the boys, my heart
settling when I see her laughing
at the fear she left somewhere above.
Later the boys try to swim across
the river on a pink plastic raft,
the placid green surface hiding
the stiff current stronger than their
teenage pride so they drift helpless
downstream barely grabbing the middle
stanchion of the bridge, working across
to finally sprawl breathless on the bank.
Our courage comes from that pride
and inexperience, our caution the only
wisdom we have to offer the young.
At four a.m. my wife and I climb out
of our sleeping bags again to head for
the restrooms, stumbling along

the asphalt path but stopping to give
a skunk wide berth as it waddles by
in the close cool blue early air—
a little time now to ourselves before
the deadening heat of midsummer steals
all we have left to face the day.
In that heat my son will sit on the bank
 reading while his friends fish for
for smallmouth bass. He looks up
as they call out to watch the rattler
zigzagging upstream with its head
an inch above the purling surface.
So it is we live with what's with us,
in the water or along the banks,
close enough to see what we have
in common, and, if we're lucky,
sometimes where the danger lies—
before it's too late and the words
we hoped would slow down the time
we have together no longer suffice.

Red-Tailed Hawks

I

I haven't the heart to tell you what I see, what we have in common with the red-tailed hawks, perched on the highway signs along the Columbia Gorge, where an ice storm can coat a semi and seal it tight. The driver sits over a cup of coffee in a diner that modestly profits from the wind's rage. We live encased in the sad rhetoric of our times, songs of love without an object, images empty of the blood we share.

II

The Ethiopian taxi driver tells me on our way in from the Nashville airport that his country's troubles all stem from the power no one is willing to share. There is too much heartache in the world we agree. All we have to do is report what we hear—the assassinated Somali poet whose son first heard him by purest chance on a reporter's tape fifteen years later in Lewiston, Maine. The dead wait for us when we've run out of things to say.

III

By what right anymore can I say I am with you in the long lines to buy water in the new deserts and sudden floods? What can I tell my children they don't know already? Their middle school friend Adam ran away in his grandfather's truck, with his grandfather's rifle. How soon the earth reclaims its own. Let us say all we have in common is our longing, like the black branches outside the window scrapping the low, gray sky.

Eastern Oregon Triptych

I

As I drive a hundred miles to the next state to see a heart specialist, I can easily take in the wide empty spaces of eastern Oregon, where today even the long rolling hills green with six-inch tall spring wheat seem impermanent.

II

Just outside of La Grande, headed to Ontario, I saw a coyote standing straight and tall in the middle of a small fenced-in herd of cattle. The cows seemed oblivious, grazing in a scattered circle around it. The calves stayed near their mothers, whose bulk perplexed the coyote thinking about what to do next, frozen by hunger, need, and the odds against him.

III

How far I've come to write this. The Imnaha running steady and clear on a lucent day, while I sit next to it in my blue camping chair. Nearby the water eddies while these words from my fountain pen lay peeled blue black on paper bright with the sun. The white water is wide here, the white noise drowning out the empty phrases, the failure of words.

Collocation

—Memorial Day Weekend 2008

We had gone to Eugene to see our son run the final leg
of a four-by-one relay—it was an eight-hundred-mile trip
for his eleven seconds.

On the way down from Portland on the interstate,
an orange muscle car, back window filled with an old woofer,
driver on the cell phone, slid, without signal, right into our lane,
the driver never the wiser—for us time only to brake and to let it go.

Coming back, sparrows were in my lane collecting bits of straw
while I was doing seventy—they took off as you'd expect but one
turned toward us and we heard it hit the bumper and then the front tire
thump over it, so I slowed down a bit.

A hundred miles later just outside Hood River I moved into the left lane
to pass a slow car and suddenly there was a green minivan on my tail.
I moved over as quickly as I could but as the van passed us at eighty
it swerved into my lane forcing me to the shoulder.

Eighty miles later flares warned us out of the fast lane. As we passed by
we saw the nine-hundred-pound boulder at rest next to the concrete meridian.
Any sooner and it would have been our last holiday on the road.

Close Encounters

While walking my dog over the high school track, past the low fence, and onto the field at the adjacent elementary school, two boys run by headed to the new jungle gym. The younger, a husky seven-year-old, stops to look back at me to say dogs are not allowed on the school property. It's the first I've heard of that rule in the six years I've been walking my dog there, so I say, *I'm bringing him in!* His is a world of rules so without hesitation he declares, *You have to keep him on a rope.* Just to give fair warning I say, *I'm letting him go*, and I slip the leash off my golden retriever to let him run free, as I do every night. The boy looks perplexed, as if it's not quite so clear anymore how the world works, but soon rushes off toward the metal climbing bars and bright yellow slides, where all you have to watch out for is the law of gravity.

The next day, a warm day in August, walking home with the dog, a dark, five-year-old Hispanic girl crosses the street—without looking but wearing a bicycle helmet—to stop us and ask if she can pet the dog. I have him sit and she rubs the top of his head. Hers is a world of questions: *What's his name? How old is he? Where do you live? Who lives there? How old are your children? They can drive? Where do they go? What's that white stuff dripping from his mouth?* She notices that the black pigment of his floppy jowl suddenly turns to bright pink inside his mouth, along a clearly demarked line, which now hangs outward while he pants. *What's that pink on his lip? That's just his gums*, I say. For some reason, I add, *We're all pink on the inside*—maybe the only thing I'm sure of. As she pulls at her lip a bit, I tell her it's time to get the dog home.

Religious Studies

The high school tennis star asked my daughter to the prom last spring but she had to decline because her college-aged boyfriend got jealous of how much she danced with the high school football star at the Fall Ball, even though she had cleared that date with him first and he was only going on what someone had told him about how close they were when dancing, someone looking to make trouble, as he should have known. Of course, the first lesson of dating is that the heart is not rational, but that's lost on true believers. Now, my daughter decides it's finally time to break up with the boyfriend so she can enjoy her last year of high school without him hanging around her neck like some medieval collar. However, by this time, the tennis star has already found another date. But news travels faster in a small school than twitter, so the basketball star steps up to invite her to the prom, they're just friends and all, although he has had his eye on her for some time. My daughter happily agrees. They double date and my daughter and her girlfriend get our permission to spend the night at another girl's house after the dance, only to discover both boys and girls will be spending the night and the father—the only adult in the house—has gone off to a bar and may or may not be seen again. That's a big *NO!* from us, so my daughter gets dropped off at her girlfriend's house, her parents settled in for the night, and we think that's the end of it, but three boys swing by in a big red truck—their dates had ditched them—and somehow the girls get permission to go out driving with them, leaving us thinking, *What the hell?* The five are in search of another boy and his date parked somewhere so that they can surprise them—the why of it a sorrowful mystery I can't fathom. Hunger strikes the girls and once they get some food, only then does the young driver say, *You can't eat that in my father's new truck.* Now the girls are sitting with slowly sogging tacos and they ask what they're supposed to do. But these are good Mormon boys so one of them has the keys to the local Church of the Latter-Day Saints, where they go to eat in the dogma classroom, in the back. While the girls sit in the small desks, the boys are at a loss. They settle on serenading them with church hymns, a cappella, with their best harmonies, while the girls finish their dripping food. When our daughter finally returns to us the next day, her one comment on the evening is a simple, *Strange*, but I'm thinking it's a miracle.

Olive Vine Necklace

–for Hannah

It rains a lot here
the leaves hold the river
you running along it
breathing the deep olive green.
We make the world by living in it
kneading our tears
our friends find and lose us
while we carry what we can
from one day to the next
against the odds—
clean needles for the Tenderloin
a food bank for campus
values seminars for men
incarcerated for life
your helmeted head
banging the cliff in the rapids
of Costa Rica, one wrong stop
in Buenos Aires. . . .
Darling, you have arrived
here with us to do what
good we can together
the only light the light
in your eyes reading
through a cathedral of books
El Ateneo Grand Splendid
the world's best bookstore.
Only ideas can save us
and what you have to offer today—
now, for the moment,

all your hard work is done
this silver necklace of peace
is entirely your own.

In the Blood

—for Dylan

Lately, I've been telling friends how my son in the first year of his computer science major took a philosophy course to round out his schedule, and had to say, in his first paper, he couldn't contradict Schopenhauer's view that pain is a positive in life—is what we all have in common—while pleasure is the negative—the party we throw ourselves when pain abates for a time, gives our due, arbitrarily, to someone else . . . and it reminded me of a visit home thirty-five years ago, after my first year of graduate school, when in order to afford a pound of ground round once a week, I became a grader for a professor teaching a course in continental literature where we read *Magic Mountain*, so that at home when I told my mother that it had become my favorite novel, out of the blue she declares of my father, about whom I knew nothing since he drank himself to death when I was nine months old, that it was his favorite also and here's his first edition, pulling it out of God knows where, after all that time.

Epithalamion for Ann and Mark
—*February 16, 2008*

In the dry summer hills you see degrees of rust stretch
across the long miles. You make your way through steep passes,
red-tailed hawks hunting for small game a hundred feet above
    as you finally find the covenant greens fed by the veiled stream.

Closer to home you see all the way across the channel
to the deserted islands where everything is carried in and a guide
is needed to show you the little that can be found—
    at your feet the ocean still offers what's left of the moon.

Now you stand here surrounded by the last avocados
hanging in their pairs, waiting for you in the soft light
and of course the fog that ripens them for harvesting
    so that you will know how the earth conspires to feed you.

You must find your way together through the hills to the clear water
you can't always see flowing and through the salt waves to float easily
in the sun that's promised even though you only promised yourselves
    that you will do this together, for now, for as long as always lasts.

San Juan Island Respite

In a long car-line for the ferry to Friday Harbor, I saw a blue heron
riding the moist current, its neck tucked in, legs floating behind.

Well before docking, I caught a glimpse of a minke whale, the short
gray dorsal speeding away from us and the noisy churning of the diesels.

Coming slowly into the dock, a motorized dingy with three girls sped by,
the brunette holding onto the outboard, thrusting her hips gracelessly

side to side. They came back for another run, the blonde mooning us
as they skimmed into the usual irreverence of the young who don't yet know

what's at stake or what to look for in a world not watching us. Over Dream Lake
a bald eagle was hunting a hawk, the two trading arcs over the dark blue

water. The eagle sought purchase, but the hawk flew upward in tight circles,
tiring the larger raptor, which gave up and wheeled out to the west to hunt

for easier prey. At Lime Kiln State Park observation point while I searched
the horizon for the promised orcas, directly below me a Harbor seal floated

on its belly, head angled comfortably just above the waterline, mottled torso
arched downward, the rear flippers folded deftly backwards together in prayer.

Just between Us

At 21° the highway through
Ladd Canyon is an even plane
of milky ice—the fog just about
breaking up below a cobalt sky,
a field for the cold sun to sit
white and distant, while below
scattering mist is caught
in a hollow, alice blue
dressing the rocks and ice. . . .
One year on an ice bridge
over Hurricane Creek,
we saw high above us
in the saddle between
two peaks the concave
knit together the unseen—
a cloud shaping right there
rising as if from solid rock
pouring *up* the mountain
to spill over the summit
toward the empty bright sky—
somehow from the distant light
and water vapor that only now
we see was there all along.

The Rhetoric of Bees and Stone

—for George Venn

I like to think we all inhabit the same Cascade landscape as George—
    with its granite, salt, and pine, sharp peaks and characters,
perhaps too these last minutes at Cape Lookout where I watch

the sunset turn the evergreens rose and the sea settle for once.
    Certainly it's Catherine Creek George saved from damming.
I've walked the southern trail with my ten-year-old son finding

the rare wild chocolate orchid to photograph for his handmade book
    of eastern Oregon wildflowers we collected in sixth grade.
I remember when the flat moist bank flew off bright yellow in spring

as with each step I interrupted the mating frenzy of five hundred
    Orange Sulfurs, butterflies no bigger than a quarter.
My children were content there to tangle their lines and catch nothing.

I have driven the Columbia Gorge these past twenty years of work
    and only now spotted the Big Horn sheep whizzing by at 70
just a glimpse of what George knows as well as the blue-tiled roof

of that final house he built by hand or the tight slip knots to hold the dying
    beech branches of the tree we had to take out in the side-yard
of our pink house, the third home our family tried to make here.

George says he likes to think of me as he first saw me when
    I had just moved to La Grande—framed in the front window
of our clapboard rental on Gekeler Lane along the Oregon Trail,

where I sat hunched over studying by candlelight, and where
    in the stony yard weeds hardly grew but my son took his first steps
near the running creek we had to make sure didn't take him from us.

Born to read, my wife and I still hunt for the contemplative life here
    amid the yellow jackets and blue hills—our quiet background
for George's rhetoric of wind and stone and redemptive song of bees.

II. Week of Days

This White Monday

Pale clouds sit so low
the foothills are all that's left
of the mountains across the valley—
little to show, the small victories
of the poplars holding onto
a handful of leaves,
so hard-won, the sun so cold
you and I don't belong here
but someplace well south,
palms and lagoons glimmering,
as if we could leave ourselves
behind and not always return
to a winter slow to withdraw,
settling bone-deep into March.
Waking each morning,
I try again to piece together anything
that's ours from the debris
of the night, only the gray skim
of work to keep the past at arm's length—
a small laugh across the room—
and now just these empty hands
to offer one another, this late . . .

Today is Tuesday

for my elephant announced
my three-year-old Saturday
morning decades ago now.
What did she know to pronounce
a sentence not heard before?
The phonemes and the words,
a prepositional phrase
requisitioned from who
knows where. Her play
translating the Tuesday
daycare trips into a scene
with her articulated
small brown wooden elephant
on four blue wheels trailing her
faithfully to fire wonder
at our time together, some-
thing crystalline to keep our
lost days—blending all that's
irretrievable except through
the language that shapes it
and holds it close.

Any Wednesday

I'm sorry your life turns
to poetry in my hands.

Not much to look at here—
white caps and spindrift,
the gulls hunkered down
like a convention of Shriners
in a small town.

The wind is raising goose-
bumps even in mid-July.
We see the edge of the failing world
with the tide running to zero.

Why should this Wednesday be
any different on the sunny
southern coast north of LA?

Thursday Letup
—for Jim Benton

2 *Undercrown* cigars
2 Manhattans—
my uncle's recipe 3-2-1
Canadian Club sweet vermouth
dry vermouth   touch of bitters
a Maraschino cherry
a little red juice ...
content for 2 hours
surprised by peace
and some understanding—not
the Big Understanding but
just the leaves budding
feeding our last appetites
for the gray final haul
after trying to make ends
meet for the last six decades
our old friends now left counted
on one hand leaving some room
for our two grown children—
having made it this far
a life of endless work
where I wasn't good
for anything but reading
and writing—a soft legacy
no one can name—
I am lucky I know
sitting here now on a white
Adirondack, the front porch
east facing the Eagle Caps—
snow fluorescing before me

in blameless early spring sun
with my drink and my cigar
to see me through

Carpé Friday

—for Susan

Let's assume this day is ours like
a Friday when nothing is due
and we can slip away
no one the wiser.

This is our time to see the hills
rolling green up to the tree line
the pines building steadily over
the last ridges.

Even doing the dishes no chore
if from the window the last snow
huddles pure white in the deep shade
above us.

With nothing pressing we can see
one another again like we
used to in the short days before
work week years

Built slowly our separate rooms
of care and the old house drifted
down toward the brown purling river
losing plumb.

But it doesn't have to be spring—
if the gray and wet closes us in
there is comfort in quiet and
a warm bed.

Today our worries can surely
wait another day. For now
can't we at last afford what
should be ours?

Saturday Last

at Riverside Park
the Grande Ronde
swells toward flood stage
trembles the steel walk bridge
the dizzy brown water below
swollen with the unmoored past
with something bad for the present—
a body floating down river
seen then unfound unnamed—
the snowmelt and spring rain
flooding Red Bridge Park
20 miles upstream while here
the ranting water slaps the banks
that can just hold their own—
we've walled away what's gone
now holding onto what we can
at least for the time being . . .

Sunday Evening

I do not understand my life
when it goes well—
salmon swimming
upstream one last time
to rest one side up
red and leaden
one empty eye to
the uncaring sky.
I'm happy enough
for the moment
with what tastes good
this evening—a glass
of champagne and crackers
then some Pacific cod
two pieces of baguette
with butter—that's all.

My dream state is at risk—
it conjures its own paperwork
meetings where I sit alone
convincing the empty chairs
of those who know better
than to try even one more time.
All in such sharp relief there
is no real difference
between sleep and waking.
I pity my own subconscious.
Morning and we wonder
why we get thirty emails?
Already there is something
I want back
more than anything.

III. Declension

Catching Up with Evolution

November 24, 2009

Dear Charles,

Congratulations on the 150th anniversary of your *Origins*, my origin already six and a half decades back. I can count in decades now, a quarter century when I need to, but no wiser. I can say, *A half-century ago I made the same mistake.* In college I would say, *I never make the same mistake more than three times in a row.* That gave me room to operate until the last dog was hung, as my mother once said. Isn't evolution a series of mistakes, the best ones taking hold, until they run out too? My father didn't last this long. I shouldn't be here now. You took the long view. Things change. I get it, I really do. It seems I've outlived my species. Those in charge hurrying things along to the end, taking all the money—no one is safe. We should have done better. You'd think we'd get the message. Instead it's statin this and levothyroxine that. Some fish oil for old time's sake. I hope this finds you well and you like it where you are. There's comfort in old bones I guess—there is no doubt now where they're headed. But this is it, except for who comes next. They're welcome to it.

Entirely yours,

More Please

Bonga
Shangase
my friend
teaches
in a
coal mine
in his
homeland
Qua
Zulu
Natal
chalkboard
schooling
so I
sent reams
of paper
250 pens
students
sent notes
of thanks
and asked
could I
please send
windows

Middle Two Rock Road

Jogging the country road outside Hershey
through Pennsylvania's early fall
I came across a groundhog stiffening
in the last warm days—roadkill
I tossed by one leg into the dry field.
It bounced thoughtlessly as I kept
running through the late afternoon
toward home, thinking of nothing
so much as the reports I had no desire
to write as I passed by the large square
houses that served as dormitories
for the boys and girls who still wound up
in the Hershey orphanage, where
they learned the value of hard work
in the fields and barns whose only
function was to teach them how much
there is to do with your bare hands
in the abandoned world.

Simultaneity

In the spring, just before Easter, the La Grande School Board voted 4-3 to ban the performance of Steve Martin's *Picasso at the Lapin Agile* at the high school. Although a number of those speaking in favor of the ban at the board meeting suggested it might be staged at the local university instead, the college's president also banned the play. She did not want to countermand the dictates of the La Grande superintendent nor alienate the conservative members of the La Grande community, after working so hard to restore relations after the debacle of the previous administration. After the campus College Democrats offered to sponsor the play, and the president found out it would be illegal to prohibit it—that bothersome free speech thing—she had to allow it but said no university funds could be used and that the students would be charged a facility fee. After the sold-out performances, the president herself led a prayer vigil to restore moral peace in the valley—on the steps of the campus building housing the theater. But at least we then knew the exact price, in dollars and cents, of free speech.

Like many members of my community, I prayed on this question. And, much to my surprise, Jesus answered my prayers. I asked Him what He thought of the local case of censorship and He said He found it *reprehensible and repugnant. Strong words, Jesu*, I responded. At the school board meeting, an elementary school principal declared that, speaking only as a father, he felt the play would rend the moral fabric of the community. But Jesus pointed out that the town's moral fabric was torn long before any student ever read this play. After all, there are over twenty teenage mothers at the high school— and a couple barely teenaged mothers-to-be at the middle school. There are over a hundred homeless students. People in the community are low on heat, food, coats, shelter. Citizens are turning in their pets at the Humane Shelter because they can't afford to feed them anymore. The local Christians really believed kids would have more casual sex because of a play. *That's nonsense*, Jesus simply asserted.

I hear Ya, Lord, but people will have a hard time believing that You told me to tell them to mind their own damned business.

But Jesus just said, *I'm speaking as clearly to you as to any minister in town. Who's to say I'm not?*

Song for the 1%

when you are gone
I go into your house
use the toilet

eat off your dishes
and put them back
without washing them

I take a dip in the pool
swimming and pissing
in your investments

didn't read your books—
couldn't find them
borrowed a cigar

in college I dated your
daughters to the dismay
of their thin pale mothers

don't worry—nothing
happened the odd English
major their modest riot

picked up your garbage
one summer even worked
the drive-in each day

harvesting empty cups
flattened popcorn boxes
your tarred butts

I delivered milkshakes
to the anorexic
at a children's hospital

cleaned floors, sugar trays
at closing time
in a doughnut shop

happy for gas money
a foreign film
cheap quart of beer

soon we'll be together
talking about the old days
as if it all were fine

but now wherever I walk
I see in the brown grass
the spines of the hungry

How It Is

Yesterday I showed up to a meeting
twenty-four hours early, while the night before
I was ready to meet a couple poets for dinner,
but I was twenty-four hours too late.
Sometimes in the morning
I need to brush what hair is left
and I take out the brush from the cabinet
bringing it down on my head—
handle side down so that I end up whacking
my bald crown with solid mahogany.
Saturday, I went shopping with my son
and I found my favorite shirts on sale;
I took one to show him—
What do you think of this one?
He looked at it, then at me, then at it again.
Dad, that's the shirt you have on.
Just today I dropped my toothbrush
and caught it by the head down at my waist
which somehow flicked the plastic handle
back so that it gave me a sharp thwack
right on the tip of my deflated dick.

The Same Coin

While walking my pet suitcase around the Vegas concourse, a model pulls me into her tent with nothing more than a smile. Thinking I will get a sample of pricey cologne out of it, I follow where she offers an instant under eye wrinkle remover trial. I'm suspicious but I'm courtesy-, beauty- (her beauty not mine), and desire-trapped (my desire not hers). She removes my glasses and can't help but softly utter, *o my*. She applies the cream under my left eye rubbing it in and says the small tube in her hand is $750, and when she sees me gobsmacked adds, *but it lasts two years!* I couldn't leave fast enough while she wanted to do my other eye to even things out. The skin under my left eye kept constricting for the next half hour and I wanted nothing more than for it to go away and leave me as I was.

Walking down Second St. past the middle school, I see a class of energetic fourth graders from the elementary school down the block lined up at the corner ready to cross to my side as I turn left on L, heading to work. Why they are rushing to the middle school is a mystery but their teacher, after having them wait at the corner, said to be careful of the man walking. As they scuttle by, I call out *Yeah, don't knock over the old man*. The boys in their exuberance rush by *okay!* But a ten-year old girl says, *You don't look old*. And I immediately thought I should turn back home because I knew the day wasn't going to get any better.

What's Coming

I snap shut the blue tub
of cut strawberries for
the fridge but instead walk
them to the rear bedroom
and open the back door
where I don't see a shelf
as my wife laughs in bed. . . .
Pausing for another
pit stop on the way home
I check my front pocket
for the car keys and find
the gum I meant to toss
then it's back to the trash
leave the gum, get the keys
this is how it is going to be. . . .
Our chancellor now wants
the fewest courses possible
for the largest number—
cutting programs, even
ones making money: film,
sculpture, religious studies.
The numbers don't add up—
nothing really left for anyone
since two Harvard economists
couldn't do the math.
The poor now fill
the beaten streets,
the thoughtless rich
voting against Health Care
and school lunches.
At this age my eyes are

improving while the rest
of me is flagging, so
I can see what's coming.

IV. The Way of the World

Entrance to Paradise

—Portland Art Museum, June 2011

I never saw a forest that does not bear the mark or sign of history.
> —Anselm Kiefer

I drove five hundred miles to see a single painting. I went north as the last mist faded from Meacham Pass at 7:00am, a band of cool blue shadow winding through the green hills below. Then west along the perpetual Columbia, eventually to Mt. Hood, its peak—from the distance—cloud-white in the cloudless sky, and found Anselm Kiefer's *Entrance to Paradise*, tucked awkwardly in the breezeway between two wings of the Portland Art Museum, four vitrines, each over nine feet tall and thirteen inches deep, steel framing the scorched woods, charred bark peeling out to reveal the blood red beneath. This was Kiefer's own *Schwartzwald*, the Black Forest near his 1945 birthplace, now bearing the full weight of history's flames—these are the gates of heaven, brambles, like Dante's outside Jerusalem—that fallen city—running across the floor of each deep frame, in front of the blistered trees in the middle ground, a wide, gray ribbon of ashen film twisting across the bottom third of the first three frames to give out weakly in the fourth, its faded images nothing more than emulsified memories. The woods gradually open in the last frame—the tarnished white of the background beckons *if only*, while we make our obstructed way left to right gracelessly, pausing at each frame so that in the final cabinet, from the proper distance barely available in that narrow hallway, the glass captures your image while the dark shredded trunks reflect nothing, so that you look back at yourself from behind the bleeding trees, as if you had already arrived at our pale heaven, beyond the common detritus of our fate, staring back into this failed world, where you remain.

Early

we like to tell ourselves
that it's wisdom when
you're still young and think
the world can keep its promises
like the immense bridge reaching
across the bay on red stanchions
solid against the faithless sea
for now we hold next to nothing—
I learned early there's little
you can you do if who you are
is not enough there's no pleading
like the time my first wife
and I were dividing
what was left of what we had
loved together she asked *why*
are you being so nice to me
to which I simply had no answer
and she went on to say her loss
was greater and perhaps at that
moment there was no better
love between us in the decade
since we had married and almost
immediately went our own ways
floating toward the unknown end
of all our differences the choices
made in the beds of lovers where
we thought we had found answers
to the questions we didn't know
to ask one another seeing
all the ways it could go wrong

if you can stay for a decade
or two witnessing desire and
the end of desire and watching
always watching for something
that hardly ever arrives
because that's not how it happens
with no beginning or ending
just the times together for what
they're worth so even you can see
clearly for a moment before
it all clouds over and a sky
of promise lays the first snow
on the mountain to the north
buttressing the only pass out
of this small town of bare trees
then early the next morning
for no reason at all it clears
there is a stark bright blue framing
the radiant white on the pines
sometimes the mountains are all
you have after much wandering
their silence an even match for
your own when all else fails

The Panther Fire

—near Happy Camp, CA 2008

August fifth at the Iron Complex fire nine died when their copter suddenly
lost power, blades hitting nearby trees bringing down the Sikorsky,
which flipped over, catching fire as the hotshots waiting to be airlifted
back to camp had then to watch helplessly, the elements in reverse alchemy,
earth, fire, wind charring their hopes into our memory. One of those who
survived reported a burning body landing on him that he had to climb out
from under and then kick out a window to escape before the chopper slipped
down a ravine to burst into irredeemable flame.

                           We see how little there is
to count on but we are still a little unclear about what luck is and what will
can do for us. Three who died wanted to become firefighters, already captive
to the majesty of the air lit from inside, ground to sky, but for one newlywed
it was to be his last summer on a hand crew, wishing to change to lowland
business far from the danger of ever-burning trees. Three were from the nearby
Oregon university, communications majors, our words all that's left for them now.
The oldest to die just retired from CAL Fire days before, then signed up
with the Forest Service as inspector only there that day to ensure run, pilot,
and mission followed the prescribed guidelines. The wife of the Enterprise pilot
believes he was already half way to heaven whenever he flew and expects
she will see him there. One of the survivors recalls little except chanting
as he scrambled out—*I'm not dying. I'm not dying. . . .*

                                But fifty miles south
ten days before at the Panther Fire a veteran chief was scouting the burn
when it turned on him and his partner—the partner chose to sprint
through dense underbrush that the chief may have thought would trap
him so he deployed what was his last resort—his fire shelter—
woven silica laminated to aluminum for an outer shell while
inside he lay down in fiber glass and more aluminum to die

of burns and smoke. The next day an eighteen-year-old rookie
was holding a fire line when a tree collapsed on him crushing his leg.
He died of cardiac arrest on the tarmac between heliport and hospital.

My son's La Grande crew started to work that fire digging out the line
behind the dozer, my boy chopping through with the Pulaski—
half ax half hoe—with the rest of the crew behind him with shovels
and hoes to clear the brush. That day his friend, our neighbor's son,
was lookout on a mountaintop nearby—the next night the entire crest
was a single immense flame filling my son's wide pupils, firing singly
across his retinas, his mind's eye where it will never fade.
His crew had to hold the fire line standing with their backs
to oncoming flames, maybe keeping an occasional eye on them,
but the real job was watching for embers jumping the line seeking purchase,
then choking them, beating them, getting them out. When he called, my son said
he had heard a tree crest explode right behind him—a shower of glowing cinders
raining down, adrenaline making him jump and set to work where soon more
crew joined him.

        Seventeen-hour day but that night they slept deeply
on the mountainside, the ground cool, then rose early with the sun to start
mop up—stumpholing first to find any tree stumps where fire settles in so deep
it can burn for a decade or more as the heat travels through the thick roots to bide
its time in the dark earth until air finds it long after we've turned our attention.
When the crew finds a stump they dig it out with axes and shovels coldtrailing
roots to drown the heat with water from the five-gallon bladder bags each man
carries up the mountain on his shoulders above his forty-pound hip pack—water
dead weight the earth keeps calling back to itself.

Lisbeth and I

are inside in the dreary weather.
Why did I watch all alone
The Girl with the Dragon Tattoo
three times in a row?
It is what we have in common—
incapable of small talk,
murder in our hearts—
she lit her father on fire.
I have always regretted not shooting
my stepfather when I was ten
as he walked the 50 yards to retrieve
the cardboard target I shot out
with a .22 scoped rifle—my first shots
repeatedly through the bullseye
until it disappeared and then
I started working around the circle
chipping away at its interior edges,
widening the hole in the center
a shot at a time. I settled for
that piece of old cardboard
with the gaping hole in the middle,
kept it with me for a long time,
something in me unable to empty
the back of his head. My friends
referred to him as *that Nazi*,
so I can understand Lisbeth,
the need to sit in the window,
the view from her new apartment
in Mosebacke Torg looking out
at Lake Mälaren black and cold
without a ripple of meaning,

the night not nearly dark enough.
I haven't endured the brutal
anal rape by the guardian like Lisbeth,
but my Nazi massaged my seven-year-old balls
one night when no one was there.
I don't have Lisbeth's piercings or stiletto hair,
having given up pain after two decades
in our centrifugal house—typewriter,
books, beds, glassware flying toward
the walls ceiling floor gnawing
the boundaries of our home.
The police came once but
in the 60s all they would say is
It's his house when he held up
his LAPD gold shield—
a get out of jail free card.
He said he used to play tennis
with Betty Grable, had
a picture of himself carrying
Shirley Temple up the steps
of the LA Coliseum.
I see Lisbeth clearly, the way
on a bus in Boston I saw
a young man draw attention
with his rainbow spiked hair,
raccoon eyes, lipstick the color
of mold, his dark jeans hung
with thick chains, heavy boots—
the male version of Lisbeth years before
her image drifted across the sea.
What I saw was not the difference

everyone else saw but what
we knew together, as if costume
was the least of our barriers,
the effort to be wholly different
making us visible to one another.
But we bring trouble to us
like bleeding swimmers at sea. . . .
Still, our enemies do not know
what they are stirring up
with their small sad souls
surprised so soon to strike
hearts of stone.

In the Way of the World

—to Weldon Kees

You were right to get out quickly and on your terms—
it's become worse, a world of bad faith and a great sameness
that is America, pure war in the air we breathe sea to sea.
You saw it coming, and were not the last—in grad school our poet
hung himself from an island pine in the dim woods near his home
for his wife to find, searching through the indifferent forest.
Then there was the poet we visited in the hospital
with his brain tumor and anger asking us what we expected?
We didn't go back seeing that death chooses us
one way or another. Sometimes we may as well
seek it out first. The wrong ones, as you guessed,
keep going until something bigger than themselves presents
itself to claim them while the good ones simply disappear
under dark water on the coast or in the slough of a small rural town.

I dreamt the other night I missed the sharp curve
on the road home, my car couldn't hold the gravel
as I sailed over the cliff a long way down to the rising tide . . .
but I found time to say *I'm going to miss this life,*
not my wife or children or dog, not at all what I thought
I would say—the sentiment coming as much a surprise
as the fall itself since most of the time I count our losses
in the daylight hours and say there's not much for us
in the way of the world.
                              As if in mirror reflection,
a few nights later I came to bed late and waited for
all the voices to subside and the spectral swirls to fade,
while next to me my wife offered a reverse mantra of her own—
I hate my life. I hate my life. I hate my life . . .

not what she lets on, caring for us all, making ends meet,
enduring the claims on body and soul and the time that's left.

In '70 I scoured North Beach among the lurid kitsch
of glass bead curtains, tin hookahs, and psychedelic posters,
for some sign I belonged with the motley citizens of cafés
like Vesuvio's and the smoky readers in the aisles of City Lights.
But I never expected much and when the bottom fell out
I just thought, of course, and waited for it to fill again
like a slow drain backing up. Still, in the end, solitude
wasn't the problem, happy to fall asleep most nights
whatever old ghosts were waiting for me there. I filled
my weary flat with coming and going or with voices
of my own, nothing like the absences shuffling through
your deserted rooms the long night before they found
your socks still soaking in the sink; that was your note
along with your Plymouth at the end of the bridge
with the keys locked safely inside as if leaving in the midst
of things was the only ambiguity left, as if you could walk out
on yourself, seeking little more than a Mexican divorce.

I can't say what's possible from here on—Robinson
in the half-shadows, rarely at home among his things—
your photo of a silver coffee set, and two candlesticks
in eerie symmetry, with the rest of our half-hearted gestures.
I've staggered over Sunset Beach too many times not to see
the Pacific's ripping currents, no place for the wary,
surely, the bitter end of all that we desire. I've walked
that bridge fighting vertigo, pacing on the sharp edge
of a large blue space . . . it is a long way down to nothing,

whitecaps slapping the concrete stanchions of our dreary defeat,
white sails from here to Oakland cupping the wind of the rich,
an immense field of gunmetal gray eliding beneath our legs,
our feet—and the sea always the last empty word.

—*for Curtis White*

What's Close to Me

This morning I found our bird at the bottom of her cage
and immediately wondered what I had done or not done—
when did I become responsible for every living thing?

Our Venezuelan Celestial Parrotlet, Georgie, had been
with us for a decade and should have had another in her—
we had carried her with us all the way from Illinois.

Of course it was to be the children's pet to take care of
and of course they never did the daily feeding and watering,
discouraged once it had pinched a finger or bit an earlobe—

at birth the hatchlings have to be separated from the father
or it will peck at the bald heads until the chicks are dead.
I would put my finger to the cage and Georgie would nip

at it, trying to do some damage or maybe just saying
hello, but I would be sure to pull it back just in time.
I invited my sister to let the bird nip her finger but didn't

tell her to be careful of the sharp beak. The bird bit hard
and my sister looked at me as if I had planned it forever.
By now I should know how easily I can lose what's dear

just from forgetting or from failing to pay enough attention.
Maybe that's the story of my first marriage where I was
able to live quietly with little to show for eleven fast years.

Whenever I have nothing to say, something near me dies,
certainly that's what happened in the white hospital room
where my mother lay after the operation and the surgeon

said little could be done when her large intestine fell to
pieces in his hands. My sister and my first wife stayed
for the changing of the bandages on the gaping wound

but I had to leave that room, only to return to kiss her
forehead goodbye and inadvertently lean on the incision
which brought a sharp look of pain and anger to focus

her morphined eyes directly on mine and the shock
of it prevented me from whispering even a sorry for
all the pain I had caused. And I wasn't there when

my stepfather died from stomach cancer but I thought
just as well. I was a thousand miles away from
the heartache he had caused for three endless decades

of scotch, broken glassware, and flying typewriters.
But I don't know what I would have said. I never
found the right words for him or my mother or sister.

So now I've been cured of hope and just wait for the next
blow, when the sky turns a final gray, the trees flatten,
and I will once again have to kiss the dead goodbye.

Winter Light

—for Joan Wurdack 1921-1983

What was it that led to Mom's sobbing as we drove the freeway
in Seattle in '77 after watching *New York, New York*?
She just broke down in my orange VW squareback, the cries
rising out of the deep past. . . . But ours was not a family
where you asked questions you would not like to hear
the answers to.
        I had never seen her cry like that,
not even after she slapped me for dating the one black girl
in our Catholic high school—all she could say as her tears fell
was *Don't tell Bill* whom I saw blacken her left eye
and bruise her upper arms for so much less. But now
she was sobbing and I knew exactly what it felt like
to bury your head in the pillow, to scream so no one could hear.

It was probably just Scorsese's images, the nights
after the war, the big bands still on the radio, though
the film shows their days were numbered by the new time
signatures and chord changes, by virtuoso rifts in front
of smaller ensembles as the lead singers slipped
into pop to play the sad anthems of the heart—the only
marching they wanted anymore.
        Perhaps it was the unhappy story,
the old light, the mix of smiles and cruelty that stays with us—
God knows she'd seen most of it down the long decades
since she lost her first husband over the English Channel—
all that was left of him—his Bible, their wedding certificate,
one yellowing black and white photo, their smiles the only thing
shining in the flat light of California in '45.
        They never found
the B-24 let alone Eddie's body, nothing left of Mom's

first love. He's long gone now and Mom is too—twenty years
now and no one I can ask *Who was this? Who were they*
to be happy so briefly before the Great Death?

He was
the only man my Mom married although she had two more
husbands, and the second, Arthur, was my father, a hopeless
drunk leaving her and a daughter to themselves in '46,
his hair having gone white in a matter of months
when he tried to engineer the last of the great gray battleships
out of the black steelyards of Pittsburgh . . . was it for these unlucky
husbands that my mother wept thirty years later as we drove home
suspended on the overpass gaping at Seattle's dark port and the cold sea
beyond?

She had followed Arthur west to California, a forlorn man,
who my sister says once held me up to the warm winter light
seeping in through the narrow windows of our beige trailer
in Culver City, a man who begged money from his best friend
to hunt for jobs in LA, spending every borrowed penny
in the dives downtown, while my mother slowly moved up
through the vast secretarial pool at Atlantic Richfield
to assist at last her friend the vice president.

Arthur left
her a final time as she dutifully took the bloody rags
my sister can still see vividly to the small kitchen
to rinse out and use over again, his kidneys and liver wrecked
by six-bit scotch.

But Mom drank her share of scotch with Bill,
that last husband whose cruelty was his only art, which outdistanced
Jimmy Doyle's in *New York, New York*. From Bill she finally got a ring
and the lie they told me when I was twelve—a wedding chapel

in Santa Maria, sixty miles north— but there was no marriage certificate
in her keepsakes we found hidden among the towels after she died.

There was plenty to cry about but nothing before or after welling
so deep, until she sat that day after another radiation treatment
in her long brown double-wide in Santa Barbara, the sun flooding in,
after I had to stop that same VW on the shoulder of the highway
so that she could open the door and throw up on the way home.
She sat in the naugahyde rocker weeping, *What am I going to do?*
What am I going to do? And for once I somehow knew what
I was supposed to say, *It will be all right. It will be all right.*
Of course she didn't believe me, I didn't either, but it was all I had.

In the end I don't know how well I knew her. I know next to nothing
about Eddie, maybe less about Arthur, too much about Bill,
the stepfather whose rage is as red as a slap across the face
in cold weather. She told me often what I meant to her
but the stories of her early first love and her own times are gone
with her—the words, the past, lost like ashes in the winter light. . . .

Stepping into Nothing

My retriever's cataracts
leave just shadows
on the periphery.
I walk him down
the front steps—
on his right
the retaining wall
on the left
I walk next to him
holding the leash tight
in case his back legs fail.
He holds out a paw
not knowing what's next
memory and love no help. . . .
At leadership workshops
they first ask what we are doing
here as I do every morning
before my shower and the pills
that keep things working.
I know what I'm doing
on the floor as I stretch
the bad leg to brace the muscles
holding my kneecap in place. . . .
It is not all that different
from stepping into the office
in the dead of winter,
a cold leak finding its way
from the roof through the floor
above to crinkle the to-do list
for the day—we shouldn't rely
on my memory since

there's nothing there
except the pink shards
on the white fireplace
mother's budding shiner
books of the month spilled
across the entryway. . . .
Sometimes there's just enough
beauty to keep going
perhaps a frigid wind rocking
the decorative grass
outside the doctor's window
as I wait to hear exactly
how much cancer there is—
but not a clue as to how long
I'll last for whatever's next . . .

V. Poor Weather

Even Now

I remember sitting in your yellow basement apartment in San Francisco

    at the small wooden table at 3 a.m. that Friday and noticing the gauze

wrapped neatly around each thin wrist and asking you, naively,
    what happened.

    You said you'd broken a wine glass at the sink. I was willing to
    accept that—

those days I accepted whatever someone told me, whether or not I
    believed it.

    Belief wasn't all that important to me then. But something made
    you say *no*,

you had cut your wrists yourself, and you asked if I didn't know a
    pain inside

    so ragged that you just have to get it out. I had so little to offer then,

so just said, *no*, I didn't know a pain like that. But I could just as easily

    have said, *yes*, because I'd seen the flowering bruises high on my
    mother's arms,

and another time her black eye, which she told me, when I asked, was from
    walking into

    a metal shelf at work—no doubt that's when I learned to simply accept

whatever was said, which made it easier to pass quietly through life,
    deciding

    it wasn't worth it to feel anything, which brought me to
    that kitchenette

with you almost forty years ago. Tonight, at the dining room table,
    the household asleep,

    I'm facing the usual questions about where it all has gone, even
    middle age. . . .

I still see the white gauze tied off, knotted on the inside, which now
    I would bring

    to my lips to say *yes*, each a gentle kiss, just to say *yes*. But after all
    this time

I have to tell you, even now, that there is no one that I know whom
    I have not

    disappointed.

Asymmetry

From my Adirondack on our front porch the new spring green of the
    apple trees

    across the street whispers to me before the bright white blossoms

shout out what's coming. Next door to the north the pastel mint cherry
    tree leaves promise

    a return to what we all know will come again, ushering in

the vivid pink blossoms to completely fill our front window in the
    even squares

    of the faux panes—like grid drawing in tenth grade to divide what

we saw into manageable units a piece at a time to add up to something

    for those of us without talent to draw freehand. But something

even simpler needed for me back then—I could draw a tree using only
    straight lines

    and circles, circles for leaves, thin stretched rectangles for the branches,

a thick pair of lines for a trunk, taking honorable mention in the
    high school

    art show for no better than B+ end of term, one of two

on a report card of As. I shrugged at the fairness and proceeded to a life of reflection: Behind the apple trees and the house behind them,

a six-story towering red maple rises next to the four-story cream-colored

manor; behind our modest clapboard a thirty-foot maple

grows endlessly over our backyard—our block a for instance in this town
of trees.

After the cherry blossoms fall the leaves turn a dark cabernet,

easier to see because of what is missing—one Italian cypress now gone

after exactly half died when the city cut the roots away

on the south side where they had cracked the water main. It had to be
removed before

crushing one of us or our white minivan—no great loss there

with its failing steering and sporadic transmission. The arborist told
us ours

were the only two Italian cypresses in town, with their

three-foot thick trunks—the death of any car jumping the curb to hit
them—and their four

vertical branches stretching fifty feet. With one gone, easier now to see across the valley the alpine peaks of the Wallowas, ancestral

land of the Nez Perce band Wal-lam-wat-kain, Chief Joseph the Younger

leading them all northeast a thousand miles, chased by the 21st Infantry

for three months over the Snake, through Idaho, through Yellowstone,

captured just short of Canada and freedom, where Sitting Bull and
the Lakota

had found a brief peace. Chief Joseph not allowed to return home—

buried on the Colville Reservation just 100 miles from Canada.

Chief Joseph the Elder, who on his deathbed implored his son

to never relinquish their birthright, lies buried at the foot of Wallowa Lake,

where legend holds the skeleton headless, 300 miles

from his son. It is absence that stays with us, palpable, lasting longer than
a tree . . .

what we know in our bones—the dry epistemology of loss.

Ladd Marsh in Poor Weather

I've been coming here lately before work just to find some peace on
    the overlook—

    it's turning now from winter but still cold. The other day the glare

from the white haze in the hollow hid everything in a pale sheen. Today the
    winter geese

    look like black boats unmoored on a field of slate; yesterday

a new cold front filled the marsh, the sun unable to quite burn through
    banks of gray,

    not cold enough now for the flurries to stick, the gusting wind

rocking my car suddenly small in this weather. I can't see half of
    what's there—

    twenty years and I've never spotted the pronghorns who wander

through the brown Bitterbrush below. I still haven't seen the mountain
    goat work down

    the rocky trail that slides underneath the freeway overpass

to the river way on the other side of town, but I can say today there was a
    mottled grouse

    in the middle of Foothill Road watching me as I slowly drove by,

while last spring, as I bicycled through, I spotted six chukars nearly hidden
in the brush

and one day, improbably, a peacock with his two hens flaring

over the road for all to see. The long road can still be good to me, even on
the interstate

sixty miles west, where my wife and I saw our first pair

of blue herons riding the air side by side evenly over cottontails, parallel to
our white van.

Last night, as I was turning fifty-seven, I dreamt that I was young

again at some resort in the mountains with friends—one young woman all
blue eyes

and dark hair talked to me while the others dissolved.

We discussed how we were going to get together word by word—
patient, careful,

considerate. I awoke thinking that's how I used to be—

that's how my second marriage started when we took six weeks of talking
to decide

to move in together while we jogged two miles each day

on the firm tideline. Twenty years later I'm a better man when I'm sick
and a fever

takes the edge off so I don't have energy to interrogate the kids

or to answer snidely every question I think my wife should have
already known

the answer to as if there were some big rush to get to the end

of every small conversation in order to do what I don't really know except
sit silently

thinking of that wounded home nearly six decades ago

and the solace I still hunt for everywhere, the quiet of this marsh on a
dismal day—

the great alpine peaks across the valley hiding under the emptying

snow clouds—these wetlands where today the rain is falling steady in
long gray sheets.

About the Author

Donald Wolff has published poems and creative nonfiction in many journals, including the *High Desert Journal*, *The Montserrat Review*, *Calapooya*, *Oregon East*, *The White Pelican Review*, *ASKEW*, *basalt*, *Cloudbank*, *Gold Man*, *Miramar*, *SALT*, *Packinghouse*, and *Solo Nova*. He has appeared in a number of anthologies as well, including *The Watershed Anthology*, the *RondeDance* annual, the *Bear Flag Republic: Prose Poetry and Poetics from California*, *Writing Home: An Eastern Oregon Anthology*, and *Aspects of Robinson:*

—Hannah Whitelock-Wolff

Homage to Weldon Kees. In 2004, Wolff was a resident writer at Fishtrap, in Imnaha, OR. His chapbook, *Some Days*, was published by Brandenburg Press later that year. *Soon Enough*, a booklength collection of poems, was published by Wordcraft of Oregon. He benefitted from a month-long summer residency working on *The Epistemology of Loss*, at the Helen Riaboff Whiteley Center, associated with the University of Washington's Friday Harbor Laboratories. Wolff recently retired from Eastern Oregon University as Emeritus Professor of English and Writing.

For other titles available from redbat books, please visit:
www.redbatbooks.com

Also available through Ingram, Bookshop.org,
Amazon.com, Powells.com and by special order through
your local bookstore.

CPSIA information can be obtained
at www.ICGtesting.com
Printed in the USA
LVHW101649171122
733396LV00003B/391